PICTURESQUE
ISLE OF WIGHT

A PHOTOGRAPHIC SOUVENIR IN BEAUTIFUL COLOUR

SALMON

One of several delightful villages which lie in the interior of the island, Shorwell is sheltered by the slopes of the downs. In addition to its charming old thatched cottages, it boasts three manor houses and an ancient church said to date back to the time of Edward III.

The unchanging charm of Winkle Street is one of the main attractions of the village of Calbourne. This picturesque terrace of 18th century stone cottages, some thatched, some with slate roofs, faces the little stream known as the Caul Bourne from which the village takes its name.

Yarmouth is an attractive little resort with a large harbour set in the estuary of the River Yar and a 700 feet long pier which is popular with fishermen. Facing out across The Solent towards Lymington, Yarmouth is one of the main points of arrival for the car ferry from the mainland.

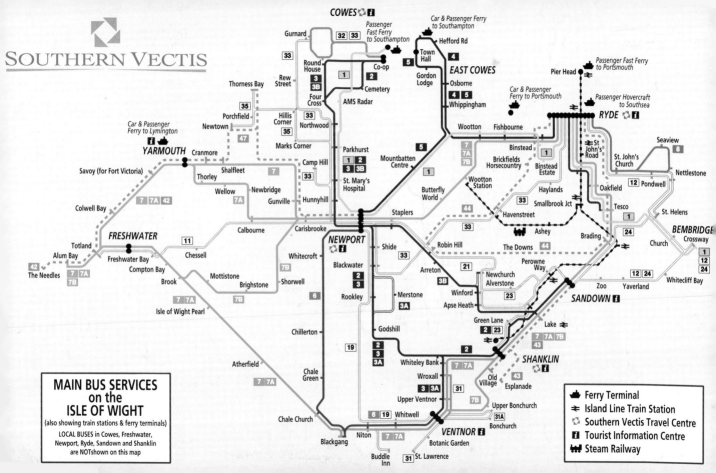

SOUTHERN VECTIS

MAIN BUS SERVICES on the ISLE OF WIGHT
(also showing train stations & ferry terminals)

LOCAL BUSES in Cowes, Freshwater, Newport, Ryde, Sandown and Shanklin are NOTshown on this map

COWES

Gurnard

Round House

Co-op

Cemetery

AMS Radar

Four Cross

Rew Street

Thorness Bay

Hillis Corner

Northwood

Porchfield

Newtown

Marks Corner

Camp Hill

Parkhurst

St. Mary's Hospital

Hunnyhill

Gunville

Newbridge

Wellow

Shalfleet

Thorley

Cranmore

Savoy (for Fort Victoria)

Car & Passenger Ferry to Lymington

YARMOUTH

Colwell Bay

Totland

Alum Bay

The Needles

FRESHWATER

Freshwater Bay

Compton Bay

Brook

Chessell

Calbourne

Whitecroft

Mottistone

Brighstone

Shorwell

Rookley

Isle of Wight Pearl

Chillerton

Atherfield

Chale Green

Chale Church

Blackgang

Niton

Buddle Inn

Carisbrooke

NEWPORT

Shide

Blackwater

Merstone

Staplers

Godshill

Whitwell

St. Lawrence

Botanic Garden

VENTNOR

Upper Ventnor

Wroxall

Whiteley Bank

Old Village

Esplanade

Bonchurch

Upper Bonchurch

Passenger Fast Ferry to Southampton

Car & Passenger Ferry to Southampton

Hefford Rd

Town Hall

Gordon Lodge

EAST COWES

Osborne

Whippingham

Wootton

Fishbourne

Mountbatten Centre

Butterfly World

Robin Hill

Arreton

Winford

Apse Heath

Newchurch

Alverstone

Perowne Way

Green Lane

Lake

The Downs

Havenstreet

Ashey

Wootton Station

Brickfields Horsecountry

Binstead

Haylands

Smallbrook Jct

Brading

Binstead Estate

St. John's Road

St. John's Church

Oakfield

Tesco

RYDE

Pier Head

Passenger Fast Ferry to Portsmouth

Car & Passenger Ferry to Portsmouth

Passenger Hovercraft to Southsea

Seaview

Nettlestone

Pondwell

St. Helens

BEMBRIDGE

Crossway

Church

Whitecliff Bay

Zoo

Yaverland

SANDOWN

SHANKLIN

Zoo

Ferry Terminal
Island Line Train Station
Southern Vectis Travel Centre
Tourist Information Centre
Steam Railway

Alum Bay, named after the alum once mined there, is situated to the north of the ridge of downs that terminates at The Needles. It is backed by steep cliffs which are renowned for their multi-coloured sands, found in nearly vertical strata on the soft, crumbling cliff-face.

Brighstone is situated a mile from the sea on the southern side of the island between Shorwell and Mottistone. Dating from the 9th century, this charming village has a number of quaint cottages and there are pleasant walks in the vicinity which make it popular with visitors.

Charles Dickens wrote part of *David Copperfield* while staying at Bonchurch, one of the oldest villages on the island. The tiny Norman Old Church of St. Boniface, only 48 feet 6 inches long, is said to have been built in 1070 on the site of an 8th century Saxon church.

Godshill is a bustling yet timeless village where neat thatched cottages cluster in the shadow of the 15th century Church of All Saints. Perched on a hill above the village, the church contains interesting monuments and paintings including a medieval wall-painting of the Crucifixion.

Popular with holiday-makers, Shanklin is distinguished from the other resorts on the island by its attractive Old Village. With its beautifully preserved thatched cottages and picturesque Crab Inn, the Old Village was originally a little fishing hamlet.

Standing in the centre of a sheltered, sandy bay, Shanklin is one of the best-known resorts on the island. With its fine sandy beach, promenade and parks, it is popular for family holidays, and also has footpaths linking it with Ventnor, Sandown and St. Boniface Down.

For centuries the cliffs at Freshwater Bay have been subjected to constant battering by the wind and waves which has eroded the soft chalk and left isolated stacks standing just offshore. In spring, sea-birds can be seen flocking to these stacks to nest.

The Isle of Wight was the last area of the UK to run steam trains in regular service and a five-mile-section has been preserved as a working museum by the Isle of Wight Steam Railway. Two of the locomotives which were used locally have been restored to their original livery.

Osborne House was built for Queen Victoria and Prince Albert in 1845 and quickly became a favourite royal residence. The grounds were laid out under the direction of Prince Albert himself and many of the state and private apartments are open to the public.

Sandown grew up around a number of forts built to defend the island against invasion from the east. Set among the old gun battery walls to the south of the town, Battery Gardens provides a welcome stopping place on the cliff walk which leads from Sandown past Lake to Shanklin.

Renowned for its mile-long-esplanade and its extensive, gently sloping sands, Sandown lies in the centre of a magnificent sweeping bay. Popular as a family holiday resort, it has a safe beach, colourful parks and public gardens, cliff-top walks and a fine pier offering traditional seaside entertainments.

Now owned by The National Trust, Mottistone Manor is a charming grey stone manor house dating from the 16th and 17th centuries. The house is only occasionally open to the public but the gardens, with their herbaceous borders, grassy terraces and herb garden, can be visited throughout the summer.

Superbly situated between the downs and the sea in Western Wight, Mottistone's ancient church overlooks the green in this quintessential English village. Some of the boulders used to build the church were carried up from the beach and the fossil remains of sea creatures can still be seen in the walls.

Brading is one of the oldest towns on the Isle of Wight, and the famous Wax Works Museum illustrates some of the characters who are associated with the island's history. The church is said to have been founded in the 7th century, but the present building is a mixture of Norman and Early English styles.

Bembridge Mill, situated on the downs behind the island's most easterly town, dates from about 1700 and last worked in 1913. The island's last remaining windmill, this fine tower mill is owned by The National Trust and has been restored with much of its original machinery.

The first lighthouse at St. Catherine's Point was built in the 14th century as a penance by a local landowner who had received goods from a wrecked ship. The present structure dates from 1838, but one of its two octagonal towers later had to be lowered because the top was frequently obscured by mist.

The famous chalk pinnacles of The Needles form the westernmost tip of the Isle of Wight. Warning seafarers away from treacherous rocks and hidden shingle banks is a lighthouse which rises 80 feet above sea-level and has a light that can be seen for up to 17 nautical miles.

Sheltered from the north winds by the island's highest hills, Ventnor is a trap for sunshine tempered by soft sea breezes. Developed in Victorian times, the resort is built on a series of terraces which give it a distinctive Continental feel; and a steep, winding road leads down to the sandy beach.

Flights of steps provide a way of exploring Ventnor on foot, and roads descend steeply past the Victorian villas which cling to the cliff-side on which the town is built. Flanked by the attractive Cascade Gardens, a road winds down from the terraced streets, round hairpin bends to the esplanade below.

One of several delightful villages in the interior of the island, Shorwell boasts three manor houses, one of which, Wolverton Manor, was built by the island's deputy governor in Tudor times. Today it is run as a working farm and is not open to the public.

Freshwater Bay became a popular residential area during the 19th century when the poet Tennyson was one of its prominent residents. Built in 1908 to serve the growing community, St. Agnes Church is constructed in the style of a barn and is the only thatched church on the island.

Seen here from Ladder Chine, on the south-west coast, the long sweep of Brighstone Bay is edged by golden sand and backed by cliffs carpeted with wild flowers. From Brighstone Down, above the bay, there are magnificent views which extend from Freshwater to St. Catherine's Point.

Colwell Bay is now a peaceful holiday beach but once it was dominated by fears of an invasion by Napoleon. Soldiers were encamped on the downs ready to repel the French invasion and Fort Albert, built in 1856 to defend the coast, still stands at the northern end of the bay.

The most easterly town in the island, Bembridge was for centuries a flourishing fishing village and commands a large natural harbour, often known as Brading Harbour. These sheltered waters were much favoured by Nelson as a mooring for the navy, but today it is popular with yachtsmen.

Wootton Creek opens out into the Solent mid-way between Cowes and Ryde. It extends a considerable distance inland and upstream there are peaceful corners where thickly wooded slopes reach down to the water. Downstream, there is a sailing school and the creek is always busy with small craft.

Capital of the island, Newport has been an important commercial centre since Saxon times. The splendid Guildhall, which stands in the High Street, was designed by John Nash and built in 1814–16. The clock tower was added later to commemorate Queen Victoria's golden jubilee.

Cowes, chief port of the island and a famous yachting centre, is known world-wide for its sailing races and regattas, especially those held in Cowes Week which takes place every year in August. From the town there are good views over the busy shipping lanes of The Solent.

The wide sweep of Sandown Bay curves away southwards from dramatic Culver Cliff, a nesting site for a wide variety of sea-birds. The cliff
is the culmination of 300 feet high Culver Down which, together with adjacent Bembridge Down, offers splendid coastal views.

South of Shanklin a cliff-top path leads towards Luccombe village, a hamlet which has heather-clad downland at its back and a rock-strewn beach with smugglers' caves at its feet. From the downs there are superb views towards Sandown Bay with Culver Cliff stretching out to sea in the distance.

The little village of Seaview stands on a prominent headland between Ryde and Bembridge. With a sandy beach, pleasant wooded walks and narrow streets and alleyways sloping down to the busy Solent, it is a popular spot for family holidays as well as for yachtsmen.

Overlooking the busy shipping lanes of The Solent, Ryde is a bustling town with many attractions for visitors. The promenade stretches eastwards to Appley Sands where the beach is backed by an attractive park with woods, lawns, gardens, a miniature zoo and pets' corner.

Ryde, with its wealth of Regency and Victorian buildings, is a major resort, the main point of arrival and departure for holiday-makers. The broad sweep of gently sloping sands make it ideal for family holidays, and well-kept gardens are an attractive feature of the seafront.